DATE DUE			
MAR 21 01			
NOV 26 01			

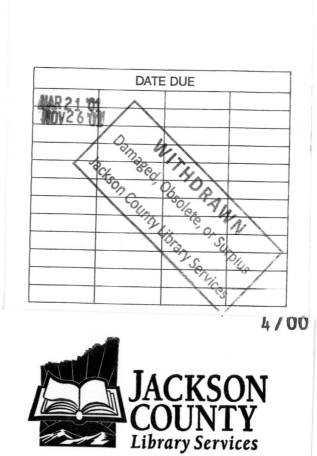

4 / 00

JACKSON COUNTY
Library Services

HEADQUARTERS
413 West Main Street
Medford, Oregon 97501

Caught in the Middle

A Teen Guide to Custody

Claudia Isler

JACKSON COUNTY LIBRARY SERVICES
MEDFORD, OREGON 97501

To Edmund, David, Julian, Evan, Jordan, and ?
Aunt Claudia loves you.

Published in 2000 by The Rosen Publishing Group, Inc.
29 East 21st Street, New York, NY 10010

First Edition

Library of Congress Cataloging-in-Publication Data

Isler, Claudia.
    Caught in the middle : a teen guide to custody / Claudia Isler.
        p. cm. -- (The divorce resource series)
    Includes bibliographical references and index.
    ISBN 0-8239-3109-9 (lib. bdg.)
1. Divorce—Juvenile literature. 2. Custody of children—Juvenile literature.
3. Children of divorced parents—Juvenile literature. 4. Parent and teenager—
Juvenile literature. I. Title. II. Series.
HQ814 .I78 2000
306.89--dc21
                                                99-044999

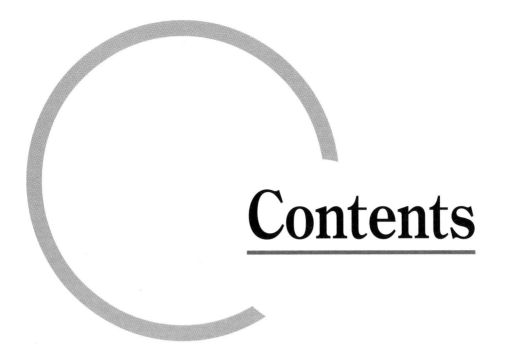

Contents

Introduction: What Is Custody?

More than one-half of all recent marriages end in divorce, and the number of divorces continues to rise each year. Every year, more than 1.5 million children are affected by divorce. For many teenagers, divorce is a part of daily life. When your parents get divorced, the first thing you have to face is how your family has suddenly changed and, in most cases, been rearranged. Maybe your mother moves out and gets a new home. Or maybe you see your father only on weekends now, instead of every evening. This new life may seem strange and confusing, and you may feel as though you don't even have a family anymore.

Divorce is frightening, and it's very painful to see your parents move away from one another. Often,

You may be getting stuck in the middle of your parents quarrels young people whose parents are divorcing feel as though they are caught in the middle. Their family is breaking apart, and they aren't sure where they belong.

No matter what the future holds, you will always have a family. It will simply look different from what it once did. The word "family" means different things to different people. Some teens live with only one parent, some live with both their mom and their dad, and some live in foster homes. Other teens split time between two homes, and some have stepparents, stepsiblings, and half siblings. These are all families; they're just made up of different people.

If you do feel caught in the middle of a divorce, this book is for you. It explains the many custody options you and your parents have. (The person who has custody of you is basically the person who cares for you and supervises you on a daily basis.) Custody options include sole custody, joint custody, visitation, and legal emancipation, to name only a few. This book will explain the custody process, how decisions are made, and how these decisions will affect your life. It will give you advice on dealing with your parents, the court system, and your own difficult and confused emotions.

Divorce isn't the end of the world, although it can sometimes feel like it. You will survive your parents' divorce. And you may even be a stronger and happier person for it.

CHAPTER 1

Sole Custody

When Brian's parents got divorced, they promised him that things wouldn't change too much. But Brian's dad moved out, and then Brian's mom rented a smaller place for just the two of them in a new town. Brian lives with his mom and sees his dad a lot, but things have definitely changed.

"It's weird not to have Dad at the dinner table every night," says Brian. "Mom and Dad always talked about everything. If I asked to go to a party or a school dance, they would discuss it. Now it's just Mom telling me what to do all the time."

When your parents divorce, you may live with one parent all the time. That parent has sole custody of you. Sole custody means that only one of your parents or your guardian makes all the decisions that will affect your life. These include where you'll live; where you'll go to school; your religious education, if any; which doctors will check on your health; what time you need to be home for dinner; and just about everything else.

The One-Parent Wonder

The parent who has sole custody and has all these responsibilities is called the custodial parent. Most of the time, the custodial parent has physical custody of you. This means that you live with him or her. The custodial parent may receive child support payments, either weekly or monthly, from the noncustodial parent. The parent who doesn't have custody of you is called the noncustodial parent. Child support is money to help pay for your clothes, food, transportation, and any other expenses of day-to-day living. Your custodial parent is legally required to spend this money on the things you need, such as visits to the dentist and school supplies.

Sometimes your custodial parent will receive additional money, called alimony. This money is intended to help support your parent, who may have trouble making ends meet now that he or she is on his or her own. The money may go toward the rent or mortgage, food,

Child support helps pay for basic necessities.

and clothing. The custodial parent does not receive this money automatically. The court decides whether your parent will receive alimony and if so, how much is appropriate. The court also chooses an appropriate amount for child support payments, if your parents cannot agree on what is reasonable. The amount of money is different from one family to the next, depending on each family's financial situation. Laws about alimony and who should receive it are different from one state to the next.

Hopefully your parents will agree on who should have sole custody of you without needing the court's help. The court and your parents are required to make a decision that is in your best interest. This means that you must live where you will be taken care of best and, as a result, where you'll be happier. Maybe your mom goes to school full-time, works late hours at her job, or has a job that takes her out of town frequently. In that case, chances are you'll live with your dad, simply because he's home more often and has more time to give you.

Division Decisions

Sometimes parents disagree about who should take care of you. In these cases, the court must make the decision for them. There are other factors the court will consider besides how much time your parents have to spend with you. Some of these are a parent's history of physical or emotional abuse, if any; whether there is a history of drug or alcohol abuse; and whether there is another adult involved with whom your parent may be having a romantic relationship.

Older kids, especially teens, often get to talk with the judge and a social worker about where they would be most comfortable. A social worker is a person whose job it is to make sure you're taken care of after the divorce. Your opinion may not determine the final decision, but it will help. If there's something you need to say, make sure you say it. Custody decisions are about your best interests, so your vote matters. Custody decisions can change too, and they can be reviewed periodically.

What Happens to the Other Parent?

Just because one parent is in charge of daily decisions does not mean that you'll never see your other parent. If you live with your mom, it's likely that you'll still see your dad, or noncustodial parent. The only time at which you wouldn't see your noncustodial parent is when that parent may be a danger to you. If your mom or dad has a history of drug abuse or has abused you physically or sexually, the court may keep that parent away from you to protect you.

In most cases, though, your parent will be given visitation rights. Visitation rights are a legal privilege given to the noncustodial parent to see his or her children regularly. This is your time with your mom or dad. Visitations often have a specific schedule, such as every other weekend, half the summer, or on specific holidays. Some parents, for example, have Wednesday nights and school vacations with their children. Visitations can be different for every family.

Visitation is different for everybody because your parents need to work out a schedule that works best for them and for you. Sometimes parents can't agree on the schedule, so the court makes the decision about what is best for you based on information it has about your and your parents' schedules. Even if you're with your mom all week, you're probably both pretty busy with work and school. On the weekend, your mom might like to spend time with you doing relaxing things like going to the movies, visiting the park, or even just hanging out together. She may want your father to have you every other weekend so that he can have some fun time with you too.

It's important for you to let your parents know what arrangements make you comfortable. Getting your feelings out in the open may help you feel better and it

It's important to discuss visitation with your parent.

may help to change things you're not happy with. For further explanation of visitation, see chapter three.

Your Rights

In all this discussion of your parents, you may wonder, "But what about me—does it matter what I want?" Yes, it does, but it's complicated. Your parents and the court are responsible for making custody decisions that are in your best interest. According to the United Nations' Declaration of the Rights of the Child, you are entitled to a childhood without adult responsibilities, a happy family life, a decent education at a school that addresses your learning needs, a doctor who knows you, a safe neighborhood to live in, and a chance to succeed in life. These are issues that your parents and the court will also look at, in addition to your physical and emotional safety.

The court may ask for your opinion, depending on your age. Not every state in the United States has the same laws. Some give preference to your desires, meaning they take into account what it is that you want, but others don't.

You may be assigned a lawyer, particularly if your parents can't agree on visitation rights or where you'll live and go to school. Be sure to tell your lawyer how you feel about these issues and why. If your opinion is going to influence the judge, this is the way to get it out there before decisions are made. This doesn't mean, however, that your lawyer will automatically do and say everything you tell her. And most kids do not get lawyers. But it's important not to feel guilty about looking out for yourself. If there is a good reason why you should live with one parent and not the other, tell your lawyer, a social worker (the court can appoint one for you), or even a school guidance counselor.

Even if only one of your parents has physical custody of you, for example, even if you live only with your dad full-time, you will still get to see your mom. She'll come to visit you and take you out to do fun things, and sometimes you'll probably get to spend the night at her new place.

Things are not going to be like they were before the divorce, it's true. But you can get used to the changes. Your family will need time to adjust to all the new demands on their time and schedules, but eventually it will work out. And usually, believe it or not, everyone is happier in the end.

CHAPTER 2

Joint Custody

"When my parents got divorced, I really didn't know what was going to happen to me," says Alicia. "I didn't know if I was going to get to see my dad, or if I'd be living with him. I was really confused and scared about the way everything was changing. But then my parents explained that they would share custody of me. I'd be moving around every week, but it was worth it to spend all that time with Mom and Dad. And when Dad moved out, he got a pretty cool place, too."

Some divorces are very complicated, but others are fairly simple. A no-fault divorce is a simple type of divorce. A no-fault divorce is a divorce in which neither spouse is guilty of breaking the marriage vows. The legal cause is "irreconcilable differences," or incompatibility, which means that your parents just cannot get along with each other. It's no one's fault. The divorce is granted because the marriage is simply over—the couple can no longer live together happily. Often in these cases, your parents will want to arrange to see you as much as possible even though they no longer live together. That's where joint custody comes in.

Two Parents, One Child

Basically, joint custody (also called shared custody) can take two forms: joint legal custody and joint physical custody. Joint legal custody means both parents share equally in the decision making regarding the child. Your parents will decide together what time you should be home from the school dance or whether you can go to that really hot concert that all your friends are going to.

Joint physical custody refers to the actual amount of time the child spends with each parent. The time may be limited (such as every other weekend with one parent) or it may be more equal (three days of the week with one parent, four with the other). Joint physical custody may help to keep your relationships with each parent strong, but such an arrangement can sometimes feel unstable. It means you have to be very flexible.

Parents who don't live together have joint custody when they agree, or a court orders them, to share the decision-making responsibilities and/or physical control and custody of their children. Joint custody can exist if the parents are divorced, separated, no longer living together, or even if they never lived together. It's common for couples who share physical custody to share legal custody as well, but not necessarily the other way around.

Why You Need a Calendar

Usually, when parents share custody, they work out physical custody according to their schedules and housing arrangements. If your parents can't agree, the court will decide on an arrangement. You might split weeks between each parent's house. This is a common

A calendar will help you to remember when you will visit each parent.

compromise. Other possibilities include alternating years or six-month periods or spending weekends and holidays with one parent while spending weekdays with the other.

Joint custody has the advantages of giving you constant contact and involvement with both parents and giving each of your parents a break from being your "only" parent. There are disadvantages, however: You may feel shuttled around, as if you can never just stay in one place. Also, if your parents cannot cooperate with each other, this can affect your daily routine, which may be upsetting. Be sure to talk to your parents about things that are bothering you. You do not need to feel guilty if sometimes you'd like to choose where to stay for the weekend, and your parents will probably let you do what you want when they can.

Types of Custody, or Different Ways Your Life Can Get Interesting

There are actually many different types of custody arrangements, and different states have different laws governing them. The most common custody arrangement, however, is joint legal custody. This is when one parent has physical custody and the other parent has "parenting time," or visitation.

There is no specific amount of visitation a court must grant. However, a typical time-split arrangement might

Legal custody: A parent has the right to make important decisions regarding his or her child's welfare.

Physical custody: The parent with whom the child lives has the right to make day-to-day decisions regarding the child's welfare.

Sole custody: One parent alone has legal or physical custody or both.

Joint custody: Parents share legal, physical, or both legal and physical custody.

Joint legal custody: Parents share the authority to make decisions about the child's welfare. They are expected to discuss and agree upon important decisions.

Joint physical custody: The child lives, on a more or less equal-time basis, with both parents. Times might alternate day to day, week to week, or month to month, or the child may be with one parent during the school year and the other during summer vacation. The parent with whom the child spends the greater amount of time may be said to have "primary physical custody," and the other party to have "secondary physical custody."

Split custody: Each parent has physical custody of at least one of the children, usually with alternating weekends and holidays, with the children together at those times.

Bird's nest custody: The children stay in the family home, and the parents take turns moving in and out, in effect visiting the children.

look like this: alternate weekends from 6 PM Friday to 6 PM Sunday; every Wednesday from 5 to 8 PM; alternating holidays (New Year's Day, Memorial Day, July Fourth, Labor Day, Thanksgiving, Christmas Eve, Christmas Day, Father's Day, Mother's Day); alternate birthdays; half of school's spring and winter vacations; and four weeks during summer vacation in blocks of two weeks.

This arrangement sounds confusing at first, but it is a system that will allow you to see as much of both your parents as possible. It's not the same as having them both in the house together, but it's the next best thing. Be sure you tell your parents if you don't think the arrangement is working, or if there is some other schedule that works better for you. They may be willing to be flexible if they think it will make you happier.

CHAPTER 3

Visitation

"I don't really like the whole visitation schedule," explains Zach. *"It's just too weird. I mean, we're not a normal family anymore, but now it's like we pretend to be one. When my mom comes to get me she's all smiles and asking me would I like to go here or there, and all I really want is for everybody to act normal. But at least I get to see her. I have a friend whose mom can only visit with a social worker along to watch the whole thing. At least my mom and I go the park and stuff by ourselves."*

Visitation is the time you spend with your non-custodial parent. This legal right is often called a visitation schedule. It is literally a schedule of weekends, holidays, and school vacations when you and your mom or dad are together. There is no law creating only one visitation schedule for everybody; they are as individual as the people who use them.

Reasonable visitation is when the schedule calls for times and places that make sense and are convenient for everyone involved. Such schedules are generally left to your parents to create. Your parents must cooperate and communicate with each other frequently for this to work.

Sometimes the court making custody decisions sets up the visitation schedule. A schedule designed by the court is called a fixed visitation schedule. The court is more likely to step in and do this if your parents are so angry with each other that constant contact between them could hurt or upset you.

In a case where one of your parents is suspected or accused of abuse, an adult other than the custodial parent must be present at all times during the visit. This is called supervised visitation. That adult may or may not be someone you know. He or she may be someone agreed upon by your parents or someone appointed by the court. Either way, the court must approve that adult.

The Legal Stuff

In some states, visitation is designed specifically to suit the needs of the children, not the parents. In Illinois, for example, a judge can't take away or limit a parent's visitation rights unless he or she finds that it would be dangerous for a child's physical, mental, moral, or emotional health. For instance, if your parent abuses drugs or alcohol, the judge will not want you to have visits with that parent. However, as long as you're safe and happy with your parent, the court will make sure you get to spend time with him or her.

The parent you live with and the parent who has visiting rights often will agree on when and where the visits will take place. But if they don't, the court will decide. The court will consider things like your age, your parents' work schedules, the visiting parent's relationship with you, the home conditions of both parents, and any special problems you or your siblings might have, such as physical or emotional conditions.

Judges will usually try to establish regular weekly or alternating weekend and holiday visitation, with a fair sharing of school vacations and holidays. Also, a parent does not lose the right to visit you because of a failure to pay child support, and a parent can't stop the other from visiting you because of a missed payment.

What About Grandparents?

A court may grant reasonable visitation privileges, in appropriate circumstances, to grandparents and great-grandparents. Over the past few years, grandparents have

Grandparents can request visitation rights, too.

begun requesting visits with grandchildren whose parents get divorced. Many states have passed laws allowing grandparents to seek a court order for visits if they've been denied visits by the parents. Some states require that a minimum period of time pass (three to six months) before the visits begin. During this period everyone can calm down and adjust after the divorce. Other courts require a hearing. If the visits are granted, the court will usually create a schedule that everyone involved is required to follow.

Each case is unique; there is no specific formula for grandparent visitation. This is a fairly new policy and one that does not exist in all states. New York, California, and Arkansas are three of the states that have passed laws giving grandparents the legal right to see their grandchildren.

Can I Visit My Stepparents?

If your mother and stepfather get a divorce, does your former stepfather have any visitation rights? Can you continue to visit him even though he's now legally out of the picture? After a divorce, your stepparent may also want to visit you. You may be very close with a stepfather or stepmother and want him or her to stay part of your life.

State lawmakers are now considering laws to help parents and kids who find themselves in this situation. Most states, at this time, don't provide stepparents with visitation rights. Some courts, however, will look at the whole picture. The judge will consider how long your stepparent has been involved in your life, your opinion about visitation, and other factors. Courts have granted former stepparents visitation with their stepchildren. Again, the bottom line is what's best for you. Remember, it's all in "the best interests of the child."

How It Works

Visitation can seem complicated because so many laws apply, but it's fairly simple in practice. If your mother is given sole custody, your father will be granted visitation rights. If your father is given sole custody, your mother will be granted visitation rights. This means that the noncustodial parent, the one who does not live with you, will be able to see you on a regular basis, with set times and days. Or it may be more flexible, depending on what your parents agree to. The court will examine the terms and, based on what's in your best interests, approve or change them a bit.

No matter what happens, there will be a schedule that your family will follow to make sure that you get to spend time with the parent you don't live with. It will take some getting used to, but after a while you'll probably like the special time you spend with each parent.

Divorce doesn't end your parents' responsibilities toward you. Each of your parents should try to play a central and important role in your life. Your parents haven't stopped loving you, and they haven't lost interest in you. They each still want and need to show you all the affection and give you all the attention you deserve. That's why schedules are created to make sure you get time with both your parents.

What Your Parents Should Do

You should be available, or ready to go, at the time agreed upon for visitation. It's your custodial parent's job to make sure that you are ready and have whatever you need for the visit. The visiting parent should arrive on time so as not to keep you waiting (or mess up the custodial parent's schedule). Occasionally, the visitation schedule may need to be changed. If one parent has made plans with you that conflict with visitation rights, your parents should be reasonable and work something out. Your well-being, health, happiness, and safety should be the first concern of both your parents.

What Your Parents Shouldn't Do

If your parent does not show up for a visit and does not notify the other parent, you'll feel rejected. Your parents should make every effort to prevent this, but try to remember that sometimes schedules just don't work out. And think about what it was like when your parent

A parent who fails to show up for visitation can cause deep unhappiness.

was still living with you. Didn't your dad ever have to cancel plans with you? Hasn't your mom ever forgotten to do something with you that you planned? It's not necessarily different now. If one parent repeatedly misses visits, however, it may be time to reassess the visitation schedule. It's not fair that he or she disappoint and hurt you regularly by missing visits.

Your mom should not use visits to check up on your dad (or vice versa), nor should you be used for this purpose. Visitation is not an opportunity for your parents to continue arguments. The visiting parent should not spend time with you if he or she has been drinking or using drugs. If you think he or she is under the influence of these substances, make sure your custodial parent knows this before you leave the house with your visiting parent.

Your parents should not make wild promises to you about visits they know will not happen. These promises make it hard to trust and respect your parents. You may see your mom or dad making promises he or she can't keep or offering things that he or she can't really afford to buy. After a divorce, a parent often feels as though he or she needs to prove his or her love for you, especially if you don't live with him or her. Make sure your mom or dad knows that you don't love him or her less simply because you're no longer living together. Spending time with your parent means more than anything he or she could ever buy you. Make sure your mom or dad knows this.

Visits should not be limited to where you live. The other parent's home; a day out; or an activity, such as a picnic or a day at an amuse-ment park, are good alternatives.

Visitation should be a time for you and your par-ent to enjoy one another. Your parent may bring another person, perhaps an adult friend, along on a visit. If this makes you feel like your parent does not have enough time to give you his or her undivided attention, try to explain how you feel. If that doesn't

Tell your parent if something about visitation bothers you.

work, talk to your custodial parent about it. Your parents should both make every effort to discuss and deal with any problems that come up.

Manipulating Meetings

Parents may agree to modify, or change, the visitation or even the custody arrangement. This modified agreement, called a "stipulated modification," may be made without court approval. If one parent does not stick to the new plan, however, the other will have no legal support to fix the problem. If one parent wants to make changes to the custody arrangements that the other doesn't agree to, the first parent must file a motion (a written request) with the court. Usually, the change will only be made if the parent making the request can demonstrate a "substantial change in circumstances." Substantial changes might be a geographic move or a change in lifestyle, such as a more flexible work schedule or recovery from drug or alcohol abuse.

Sometimes parents get worried or convinced that children belong only with them and not with the former spouse. Occasionally, a parent will break the law in an attempt to protect his or her children or hurt his or her ex-spouse. Visiting parents are not supposed to cross state lines with children without consent from the custodial parent. If you are supposed to see your mom for the weekend, and she takes you on a trip to an unfamiliar place or a trip that is longer than the weekend, she may be guilty of abducting, or kidnapping, you. The laws that apply to any kidnapper would apply here. If caught, the parent guilty of this crime faces time in jail.

If you think your parent is breaking the visitation agreement, you can try talking to him or her. You can also try to contact your custodial parent. If you can get that parent on the phone, tell him where you are and who you're with. Notify an adult, preferably a police officer, that your parent has broken your visitation agreement. It might seem mean or disloyal to your parent, but she has broken the law. Custody arrangements were made with your best interest in mind, and both parents are legally bound to follow them.

Visitation schedules are for your benefit, set up so that you get to spend time with both parents. Like the divorce itself, this schedule will take some getting used to. After a while, it will be as routine as getting up and brushing your teeth. And because the time you spend with each parent has been carefully worked out, it will feel special, like time set aside just for you.

CHAPTER 4

Foster Care

The situation in Clarice's house was really bad. Her father had left her and her mother when Clarice was five, and her mother had never gotten over it. Her mom used drugs and spent a lot of the family's food money on her habit. Sometimes, when she couldn't get drugs, she would get uncontrollably angry. She'd scream and shout and hit Clarice for no reason. One day, Clarice's gym teacher asked about the bruises on Clarice's legs and arms. Clarice felt bad, but she finally admitted the truth. "It was my mom," she told the teacher.

Not long after that, a woman showed up at Clarice's house. She talked to Clarice about foster care. Forty-eight hours later, Clarice was in the custody of a foster care worker and on her way to a new place to live. She felt so guilty about her mother, she couldn't let anybody see how relieved she was to get away.

Children all over the United States live in foster homes. A foster home is a safe place for you to stay when your parent or parents are unable to take care of you. It may be a house or an apartment with two married foster parents or a single foster parent, and they may have other foster kids or kids of their own living there. The state where you live is responsible for your welfare, and employees of state agencies decide if you need to be in foster care. The state agency that trains and licenses foster parents is usually Child Protective Services (CPS). CPS has the duty to investigate abuse, neglect, and abandonment cases. In most states, CPS provides services designed to help families solve their problems and stay together. One of these services is foster care.

Why Some Kids Need Foster Care

Why would anybody take you out of your own home? Well, sometimes when parents get divorced, they find themselves unable to care for their kids. Depression is a fairly common side effect of divorce. Depression is a deep sense of sadness and unhappiness that lasts a long time. Some adults don't handle these feelings well or don't seek therapy when they need it. A few parents

may turn to drugs or alcohol or may already have a substance abuse problem. Kids who need foster care come from families that need help. Their parents may have neglected, abandoned, or abused them physically or emotionally.

Neglect, the most common form of child abuse, can be physical, emotional, or educational. Parents may fail to supervise their children or make sure they get health care, food, clothing, or shelter. They may not make their children go to school. These are all good reasons to remove you from your parents' home and put you somewhere safe. None of them are your fault.

Your parents may need professional help to recover

Divorce can be very depressing for adults too.

from drug or alcohol abuse. Drug and alcohol abuse make it difficult to take care of oneself, let alone one's children. Your parents may also have psychological or emotional problems that make them unable or unwilling to take care of their children. It's important for you to remember that no matter what anyone says, neglect is never your fault. It's not your job to make sure that your parents take proper care of you.

If You Need Foster Care . . .

Child Protective Services depends quite a bit on responsible adults to protect the state's children. They need a responsible adult to tell them when there's a child that needs help. If you're in an unhealthy or dangerous situation at home, there are several things that can happen. You can ask for help yourself by talking to a trusted teacher, a school counselor, or a family friend. If you don't do this, but one of these people notices that there are problems in your home, he or she may call CPS to report suspected abuse. A social worker, someone who is trained to offer help to you and your family, will respond to the report. He or she will talk to the person who filed the complaint, your parents, and you.

The social worker's job is to determine the level of risk involved in allowing you to stay in your parents' home. Do your parents simply need a little help in taking

care of you, or are they actually dangerous to you? Ultimately, the goal is to keep families together or to get them back together eventually. The social worker may decide that you can stay but also that your family requires services. Services could be counseling or parenting classes, among other things.

However, if the social worker feels that it is in your best interest to remove you from your home, he or she will recommend it. If your parents agree with the social worker, he or she must take your case to juvenile, family, or probate court to discuss it with a judge. The judge will make the final decision about whether or not to remove you from the home. If the judge agrees with the social worker, the social worker will bring the court order to take you out of the home and place you with a foster family as quickly as possible.

If your parents refuse to allow the social worker to remove you, then the social worker will return with a police officer to get you out of the unsafe environment. In sexual abuse cases, the police officer that accompanies the social worker is specially trained to deal with victims of sexual abuse. This sounds like a scary situation, but it is important for you to keep in mind that the police officer and the social worker are not there to break up your family. They have come to make sure that you don't get hurt. Sometimes it is best for your

Tell your social worker about your problems.

family members to take a break from each other, particularly if a parent is treating you badly.

After you're placed in foster care, your case then goes from the social worker to a foster care worker. A foster care worker will work with your foster parents, your parents, and you to work out a contract. Parents are required to show by their actions that they intend to work to get you returned to them. They must solve whatever problem caused you to be in foster care. The contract is one in which all family members agree to accept whatever social services are required to reunite the family.

Who Is Your Foster Family?

Not just anyone can be a foster parent. Foster parents are specially trained and licensed by Child Protective Services. They have to show they have certain qualities needed to be good foster parents. They must be responsible and stable and have patience and understanding. They must be willing to learn from the experience of being a foster parent. They have to have room in their lives to love foster children. They also have to be able to let them go when the time comes for them to return home.

Foster parents don't just need room in their lives for foster kids; they need room in their homes. They have to be able to give you a bedroom, and if you're sharing with another kid, one that's big enough for everybody. (The average foster parent is licensed to care for up to three children.) Their home should also be a safe, emotionally healthy place.

A lot of people think that only married couples living in houses can be foster parents. That's not true. Foster parents can be married, single, or divorced. They can live in a house or an apartment. They can be as young as twenty-one years old and working outside the home, or they can be older, retired people. More and more often, the foster care system is turning to the relatives of children who need care to be providers of foster care. This type of foster care is called kinship care.

Foster Care Versus Adoption

Foster care and adoption are not the same thing. Adoption is a legal process through which an adult legally becomes the parent of someone who is not his or her biological child. If you were adopted, you are a permanent member of a new family, and your birth parents have no legal tie to you.

Children in foster care are generally there only temporarily. The goal is to get your family back together or find a more permanent situation for you—especially if you have been in foster care for two years or more. Your stay in a foster home could be as short as overnight or as long as several years.

At the age of eighteen, you "age out" of foster care. This means that you must move on from the foster home, either into the workforce, living with a member of your biological family, or to college. You will receive help with this process, and you will be able to talk to your case worker about any concerns that you may have. Unfortunately, this system is not the best it could be. The number of foster care agencies that provide employment-related services is limited. However, your high school may be very helpful in assisting you to find a job.

If you are adopted, your adoptive parents' responsibilities for you are the same as they would be for any biological child they have. They will help you with school and employment to the best of their ability. Your care is up to them, not to Child Protective Services.

No matter whether you're placed with strangers or relatives, you will have a case worker whose job it is to look out for your welfare. That's whom you should talk to if you're having problems in your foster home you can't solve on your own. It will probably feel strange to move in with strangers, but as you get to know them, they'll feel more like family. Your foster family is there to help you and care for you. You can talk to them about things that are bothering you—your homework, your friends, or other problems—just as you would a biological family.

CHAPTER 5

Legal Emancipation

Ahmed was taken away from his parents by a social worker and a police officer a few years ago. His father had been sexually abusing him, and his mother just wouldn't believe that it was true. Both of his parents denied that the abuse had ever happened.

Ahmed had been living with the Grants, his foster parents, for about a year. Occasionally, the Grants and Ahmed would talk about how much they'd all like it if Ahmed could become a permanent member of the Grant family.

More time went by, and after two years, Ahmed had still not seen his parents. He went to court to ask for emancipation from his birth parents. He couldn't go back to his parents' home because it wasn't safe for him. But he couldn't be adopted by the Grants unless his parents said yes or unless Ahmed was free, or emancipated. The court saw that it was in Ahmed's best interest to be away from his parents, and they granted his request for emancipation.

Emancipation means freedom. Legally, emancipation is the process through which you legally remove yourself from your parents' care. You live apart from your parents; you're not receiving any financial support from them; and you're not in foster care. You can gain emancipation in several ways: You can go to court and ask a judge to order it; you can get married; or you can enlist in the armed services. There may also be other situations in which your state's laws allow emancipation.

A court decides if you can be legally emancipated.

Running away or being told to leave by your parents is not considered emancipation. Your parents are still responsible for you and will be held accountable for your actions. If you're emancipated, your parents have no authority over you, but also no responsibility for you.

An emancipated minor is someone under the age of eighteen who is legally emancipated, or free from, her parents or guardian. Not all states allow minors to seek emancipation. Alabama, Arkansas, California, Illinois, Indiana, Kansas, Louisiana, Michigan, Mississippi, North Carolina, Oklahoma, and Tennessee are states that have passed emancipation laws.

If your state has such a law, you need to find out about it and follow its requirements. Then the court will hear your case and decide what's best for you. You may have to show that you have a job, that the job provides a salary with which you pay all your own bills, that you live in your own place, and that your parents aren't claiming you as a dependent on their taxes.

The Real Deal on Emancipation

Being emancipated comes with some serious adult responsibilities. You have to be mature to handle a lot of these responsibilities. You are entirely accountable for your welfare. In some ways, this may sound like it would be a lot of fun—you can stay up as late as you want, eat whatever you want, hang out with whichever friends you feel like. But it's not all fun, and you should consider your circumstances carefully.

Emancipation is a legal option meant for teenagers who are being abused and neglected or who have been in foster care for a long time and have had little to no contact with their real parents over that time. You'll have to take care of yourself even if you are not yet old enough to vote, buy property, or even rent a car. Talk with somebody you really trust before deciding to go ahead and ask a court for emancipation. And if you are already emancipated, always talk to other adults when you're facing a new problem or situation you're not sure how to handle.

Rights and Privileges

Different states have different laws governing emancipation and offer different rights and privileges. In California, a minor who becomes emancipated has all of the following rights and privileges:

- ❖ To seek medical, dental, or psychiatric care, without parental consent, knowledge, or liability

- ❖ To enter into a binding contract (buying a car, getting a loan, etc.)

- ❖ To sue or be sued in his or her own name

- To make or revoke a will (a document that gives instructions about what to do with your property after your death).

- To establish a residence

- To enroll in a school or college

Depending on where you live, you may not have all these rights, however. For example, in New York, an emancipated minor is still required to get parental consent to get working papers (which are needed to get a job) and is limited in the kind of jobs he or she can hold. A minor cannot bring a lawsuit and must have an adult sue on his or her behalf. The minor cannot buy or sell real estate, and he or she must get parental consent for routine health care.

In New York, the minor's rights include the right to keep his or her own wages, the right to sue for financial support from the parents if they forced the youth to leave home, the right to establish a legal residence and attend school where he or she lives, and if necessary, the right to public benefits such as food stamps.

It's clear that your rights and privileges will be different from state to state, so you should investigate your state's emancipation laws. Seeking legal emancipation is a difficult process. Make sure that there are adults you can trust and talk to about the problems you're having.

Your lawyer can answer your legal questions, but you'll need help to work out your issues with your family.

Just as it's the duty of the court to act in your best interests, it is your job, too, to figure out what might be best for you. It requires a lot of maturity to make this decision and to live with it. However, if the safest thing for you is to be free of your parents' authority, then you should carefully consider emancipation.

CHAPTER 6

Life in a Blended Family

"When my dad got remarried, I thought it would be like the movies," explains Indira. "I thought I would get this evil stepmother, who would make me do all these chores and be really mean to me and tell me what to do all the time.

"And I didn't feel right about my mother going out on dates and stuff. I mean, I felt as if I was keeping secrets from Dad when I would visit him. But then Mom met Ron, and he's a really great guy. I mean, he's not my dad, but he's fun to have around, and he helps me with my history papers. He makes my mom really happy, too. I think that I'll like it when he marries Mom."

At some point after your parents get divorced, one or both of them may begin to date other adults. It may

be time for your parents to move on and build a life with someone else. Your mom and dad may date and may eventually even marry again. It may be hard for you to accept a new person as part of your and your parent's life. But just as your parents want you to be happy, you want good things for them, too.

One Parent, Two Parents, Three Parents, Four . . .

Your parents' dating may only begin to get your attention if, for instance, Mom brings a date along with her the day she's supposed to visit you. Hopefully, she has not surprised you with the extra company. But if she has, you need to find some private, quiet time to tell her how you feel about that. That visitation time is yours to spend with your parent. If you're uncomfortable, your mom needs to know that. She may not like hearing it, but she'll probably understand. She has other time she can spend with her new friend.

Sometimes, after your parents have been dating other people for a while, one or both of them may decide to get married. There isn't anything that can prepare you for the confusion of feelings that comes when a parent tells you he's marrying someone new. You may feel you're betraying your mother if you're

Accepting a stepparent takes time and patience.

happy for your father; you may feel as if you've lost your father to his new wife. Or you might just not know what you feel.

That's all pretty normal, and you can talk to your parents about it. What's important is to talk about it calmly. All the feelings and emotions stirred up in you and your parents over such an event can make people react in fear and anger. Obviously that's not the best way to talk about things. Figure out what frightens you about the new arrangements (you may even want to write it down) and explain it to your parents. If something about it makes you angry, you can explain that, too.

What's a Blended Family?

If your parent remarries, you'll then be part of a blended family. A blended family is one that includes stepparents, stepsiblings, or half siblings. Half siblings are brothers or sisters with whom you share only one biological parent instead of two.

Life in a blended family can be tricky. You have to get used to having new people as part of your family. You'll probably even have to get used to living with a new parent or new brothers or sisters. It takes time to adjust to such a big change, so don't worry if it feels weird at first. After a while, you'll gradually start to feel more and more like a family.

A blended family can add wonderful things to your life. If you grew up without a mom or a dad, now's your chance to have one. That doesn't mean your stepmother will replace your biological mother, but you can still share a lot of special things with her. Maybe you've always wanted a younger sister or an older brother, and now you have that person in your life.

It's not always easy to be a part of a blended family, and often it's hard. But most people agree that it's worth the struggle of adjusting to the new family members. For the rest of your life, you'll have more family members to support, encourage, and love you. Who wouldn't want that?

Can My Stepparent Adopt Me?

The laws that govern stepparent adoptions are different from adoption laws for nonrelatives. If your custodial parent remarries, and your noncustodial parent doesn't visit you or support you in any way, there's a chance that your stepmom or stepdad can adopt you. Usually, the court will notify your noncustodial parent and then begin proceedings to terminate his or her parental rights. In other words, the court will work to remove you from your noncustodial parent's authority and responsibility. Once you've been adopted by your stepparent, you are legally his or her child. Unless one of your parents has died, a stepparent cannot adopt you without legal consent to the adoption by your biological parent.

In most states, a stepparent can adopt you if the absent parent gives written, legal consent to the adoption. He or she can also adopt you if the absent parent's rights are terminated in court, if the absent parent has died, if the absent parent abandoned you (left you uncared for), or if the other parent has abandoned you. Laws about abandonment are different from state to state, and you should research them thoroughly.

Happily, *Cinderella* is just a fairy tale. Your life is unlikely to be taken over by an evil stepmother and stepsisters. Like all the other parts of your parents' divorce you have had to deal with, this one may take some patience on your part. You may not like every person your parent dates, but your relationship with that parent last through anything. Together, you and your mom and dad, and even your stepmom and stepdad, can create a family life that—although different from the one you once had—can be filled with love and happiness.

Blended families can be very loving and happy.

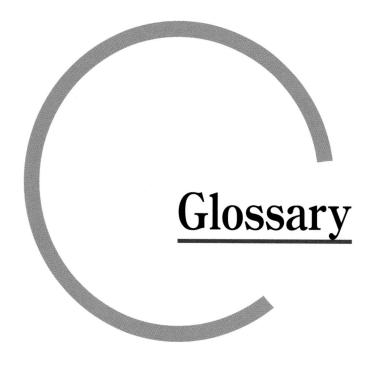

Glossary

alimony Money that one parent may pay to the other after a divorce to help pay bills.

child support Money that the noncustodial parent pays to the custodial parent to help pay for the child's food, clothes, school, medical expenses, and other day-to-day costs.

custodial parent The parent with whom the child lives.

dependent Financially reliant on others.

fixed visitation schedule A schedule of visits with the noncustodial parent that has been arranged by the court.

guardian A person legally responsible for the welfare of another person.

irreconcilable differences   Disagreements that cannot be solved.

joint legal custody   A legal arrangement in which parents share the authority over and responsibility for their child.

joint physical custody   A legal arrangement in which a child spends a more or less equal amount of time with each parent.

kinship care   Foster care in which the foster parent is a relative of the child in need of care.

minor   A person under the age of eighteen.

no-fault divorce   A divorce that happens simply because of the couple's inability to get along with each other.

noncustodial parent   The parent who has visitation rights; the child doesn't live with this parent.

social worker   A person specially trained to offer counseling services and other help to families in trouble.

sole legal custody   A legal arrangement in which one parent makes all the decisions about the child's day-to-day life.

terminate   To bring to an end.

visitation rights   Legal privilege given to the non-custodial parent to see his or her child regularly.

Where to Go for Help

In the United States

Children's Defense Fund
25 E Street NW
Washington, DC 20001
(202) 628-8787
Web site: http://www.childrensdefense.org

Children's Rights Council
300 I Street NE, Suite 401
Washington, DC 20002
(202) 547-6227

NEO Teenline
(800) 272-TEEN

A confidential, judgment-free hotline where teens can discuss their problems with caring listeners.

The Stepfamily Foundation, Inc.
333 West End Avenue
New York, NY 10024
(212) 877-3244
(212) 799-STEP (24-hour information line)
Web site: http://www.stepfamily.org

In Canada

Canadian Youth Rights Association
27 Bainbridge Avenue
Nepean, ON K2G 3T1
(613) 721-1004
Web site: http://www.cyra.org

Family Service Canada
404-383 Parkdale Avenue
Ottawa, ON K1Y 4R4
(613) 722-9006
Web site: http://www.cfc-efc.ca/fsc/

Web Sites

My Two Homes

http://www.mytwohomes.com/

A site where young people can order cool stuff to make life with two homes easier: a calendar to keep track of days with each parent, a handbook, a photo album, and more.

The Kids Corner

http://www.eros.thepark.com/volunteer/safehaven/
   divorce/divorce_kids.htm

For young people whose families are going through or have been through a divorce, with links to sites specifically for teens and sites in Canada as well.

For Further Reading

American Bar Association Family Law Section. *My Parents Are Getting Divorced: A Handbook for Kids*. Chicago: American Bar Association, 1996.

Bolick, Nancy O. *How to Survive Your Parents' Divorce*. Danbury, CT: Franklin Watts, 1995.

Jacobs, Thomas A. *What Are My Rights?: 95 Questions & Answers About Teens & the Law*. Minneapolis, MN: Free Spirit, 1997.

Kimball, Gayle. *How to Survive Your Parents' Divorce: Kids' Advice to Kids*. Chico, CA: Equality, 1994.

Levine, Beth. *Divorce: Young People Caught in the Middle*. Springfield, NJ: Enslow, 1995.

Porterfield, Kay M. *Straight Talk About Divorce*. New York: Facts on File, 1999.

Prokop, Michael S. *Divorce Happens to the Nicest Kids: A Rational Self-Help for Children, Parents, & Counselors*. Warren, OH: Alegra, 1996.

Index

About the Author

Born and raised in New York City, Claudia Isler has edited material ranging in subject from robotic engineering to soap operas.

Photo Credits

Cover and pp. 9, 18, 29, 31, 36, 38, 50, 54 by Christine Walker; p. 4 by Les Mills; p. 13 by Ira Fox; p. 25 by Thaddeus Harden; p. 44 © Uniphoto.

Design and Layout

Michael Caroleo

Series Editor

Erica Smith